THE COMP AMERICAN MONEY SYSTEM AND ITS IMPORTANCE

By Fernando Penagos

CONTENTS

Dedication

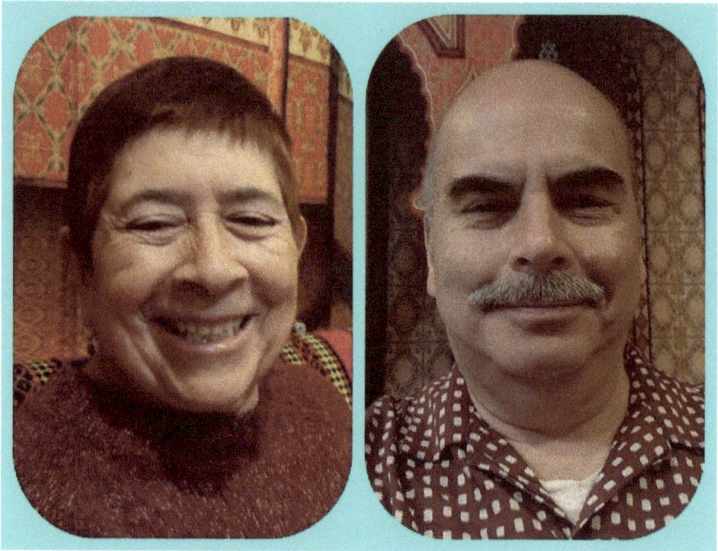

To my wonderful parents, who have been with me for as long as we can remember. For the many different times that we have been together and have spoken to each other in either English or Spanish, your support, kindness, and joy have given me the generosity and public work to dedicate this fine but important story to both of you.

You two have not only been more helpful to me in times of great need as my folks, but we have been close to one another as warm, loving friends. Let's continue doing the best we can to keep it up. The couple of you are the ones who have given me the most admiration, warmth, hospitality, and care. It's nice to have such fine parental figures who have and shall continue to love me in every way possible.

For whatever doings that I have needed guidance from you guys, as my mom and dad, I will gladly keep providing my much-needed services to you. Please let this book remind us of all the occasions that we have been together and for all the other moments that we shall continue having as a family, no matter where we live or wherever we go out for regular errands as well as big vacations.

Even while both of you can continue giving me the best support possible, you will always have a very special and touching place in my heart and memory. We will keep coming up with as much help, aid, finances, and love as possible for ourselves for the remaining times that we are completely together as father, mother, and son.

Acknowledgments

I would like to extend my heartfelt gratitude to everyone who played a role in bringing this book to completion. First and foremost, I want to thank the team that supported me throughout this publishing journey. Your time, attention to detail, and encouragement have helped shape this work into what it is today.

Special thanks to John Foster and the entire company who assisted me along the way—your contributions are deeply appreciated. I also wish to express my love and appreciation for my family. To my parents, whose unwavering belief in me has meant more than words can express, I dedicate this second book to you with honor and pride. Your support continues to inspire me every day.

To my grandmother, who deserves to be through the dedication of my first book, thank you for being a guiding light in my life and work. This second volume builds upon themes and reflections introduced in my first book. The foundation laid in that earlier work helped form the ideas that now take shape in these pages, and I am grateful to all who read and supported it. Your encouragement, presence, and belief in the message of this book have made all the difference.

About the Author

For more than 12 years, Fernando Penagos has found strength, support, and a true sense of belonging at the Somerville YMCA, a place he proudly calls his second home. Born on December 25, 1982, Fernando once faced significant health challenges, including weight issues and high cholesterol. Concerned for his well-being, a family member encouraged him to take control of his health by joining the Y.

Motivated to transform his life, he adopted a rigorous fitness routine, committing to 3 to 4 hours of exercise per session, 4 to 5 days a week. His training includes a wide range of the Y's offerings: treadmill workouts, heavy bag boxing, biking, and swimming. Among these, swimming has become a cornerstone of Fernando's wellness journey. He meticulously tracks his progress, recently completing 800 laps in just two weeks, and surpassing 8,593 laps between the previous year and July 2021.

Beyond fitness, the Y has offered Fernando a supportive and uplifting community. He thrives in the welcoming environment and credits the staff for their genuine care and encouragement, which have played a critical role in helping him stay focused on his personal and academic goals. Having graduated from Rutgers University and County College of Morris, he believes the mental clarity and reduced stress gained through his YMCA experience have been essential to his academic success.

"The Y is more than a gym—it's a vital part of my daily life. The staff truly cares about my well-being. Through the Y, I've improved my health, reduced stress, and found the focus I need to succeed. I'm proud to share how much the Y has impacted me with my family, professors, and everyone I meet." Fernando's story is a powerful testament to how the YMCA can transform not just bodies, but lives, through community, encouragement, and resilience.

Preface

This book is written by Fernando Penagos, born on December 25, 1982, and completed in June 2025 at his home in Middlesex, New Jersey. This book was created to explore the many forms, uses, and meanings of American money. It goes beyond coins and bills to include the wide range of modern payment methods now used in the United States.

The goal is to provide a deeper understanding of why money matters—not just in its physical form, but also in the way it's handled, spent, and managed in daily life. Throughout this book, readers will discover why it is important to always carry money when leaving home, whether for simple errands or important obligations.

It discusses the proper types and amounts of payment to keep on hand, the common places where money is spent, and the variety of people, both ordinary and significant, who use it regularly. It also highlights how money plays a role in everyday transactions, decision-making, and personal responsibility.

Ultimately, this book is about being prepared. It serves as a practical guide for anyone seeking to better understand U.S. currency and payment systems, along with thoughtful advice on managing money with care, purpose, and awareness.

Chapter 1
The Basics of Money

If everyone can remember, nothing in life is free. No matter what anybody truly wants or needs, it all costs money. This is always used to pay for practically anything that everyone wants or is required to have. Money can come in many different forms, but for whatever method people want to use to pay for stuff that is necessary to them, having most or all their different ways to buy what they primarily want or absolutely must need is important.

Even if a lot of citizens basically carry small amounts of cash or even any plastic cards in their wallets, it's very important that they always come prepared with all of this. Money as well as other forms of payment in the United States is crucial to every person in the United States. Currency in this country can be used to pay for quite some of people's minor needs such as food, beverages, medicine, oral needs, things for cleaning their own bodies, and anything else that they would normally purchase either occasionally or quite often.

On the other hand, money is positively necessary for paying much bigger needs such as bills and any particular or specific expenses. No matter how much anyone has in cash or even their other means of being able to pay for what they need, they must always carry it with them.

Even if a single person has his or her own flexible, steady job or any means of being able to make their own living, he or she must make sure to accumulate as much pay as possible. Additionally, they need to be careful with how much money they spend from time to time. People not having enough of this on them can lead to unexpected disasters, such as not being able to pay high bills that they were supposed to pay quite a while ago. Something like that can even result in them losing their homes completely.

No matter how every person chooses to pay for whatever they normally want or for what is very necessary for them to have, they need to be sure to carry a reasonable amount of money. They cannot be with too little or too much of it. Everyone in the United States needs to decide very wisely how much cash they want or need to put in their wallets. They must even prepare very carefully before going outside to see what they either want to buy or need to pay for.

Besides any amount of currency, all forms and methods of purchasing something minor or major must be handled with extreme care and caution. All people must also be prepared for anything unexpected that they need to use their money for. A quick example of this can be if someone wants to order pizza or any type of food from restaurants, either for pickup or delivery.

The prices for this include not only the primary amount but even any tax amounts as well as the much-needed tip. This not only goes for occasional food but for anything that can cost a lot of money, which at least includes the tax that is required to pay along with the current balance of whatever somebody absolutely needs to purchase.

On the other hand, any kids at reasonable young ages can earn small amounts of money by starting some of their own businesses, which can be like opening a lemonade stand, raking leaves, mowing lawns, or even shoveling snow for any residents in their neighborhoods.

However, it's not all that easy or even the same for adults. As mentioned before, they must make their money by having flexible or steady jobs, careers, and occupations. Additionally, whoever they work for needs to pay them an amount that is considered not too low or not too high in case there are unexpected tax issues to deal with.

No matter how many families make their living or something like that, making and earning a lot of money is positively vital for them so they can gain all the support that they need. While banknotes are the more popular means of paying for anything that all citizens want or are supposed to have, many other forms and methods of payment have been supplied to those who may be low on cash.

I will be discussing the many different means of purchasing in the next several chapters of this book. Be prepared to pay full attention to all of that because everything will be mentioned. Learn very well about American money in this story.

Chapter 2
Small Means of US($) Currency

For the first form of money that will be mentioned here, it is known as coins. The several different types of coins in the United States are broken down into the following categories. The smallest one is the penny, which is made of copper and is only worth one cent. Even if this is the lowest coin in our country, having a whole roll of them adds up to 50 cents. The penny is put in the red coin roll, which is labeled for that form of money.

Sometimes, having several of these, along with occasional cash, can come in handy if there is anything that needs to be paid for, including cents. It's a coin that can be saved up somewhat easily in a piggy bank. The same goes for all forms of coins, no matter how much they're worth. The next coin in U.S. currency is the nickel, which is worth five cents and is made of silver.

Having forty of these in their roll adds up to $2. The roll for it is the blue one. This is yet another common coin that can be used for anything that requires cents to pay for it. It's one that can be spent quite often. On the other hand, it could even be needed for minor things such as lottery tickets, scratch-off cards, and other stuff like that.

The same goes for every coin that has and still will be used for buying all important or primary items. The third coin is the dime, which has the value of 10 cents and is yet another one that is made of silver. They are put in green rolls. A full one adds up to $5.

Sometimes, there are people who believe that dimes could be considered somewhat lucky. Whether that is true or not, this is a coin that is very much used in purchasing items that include cents in their prices. Even a lot of dimes can be easily saved up for anyone who wants to start their own coin collections and all that. If there will be any items that will need to be paid for using these, it is yet another very crucial method of payment to have on hand.

The fourth coin in the American money system is the quarter, and it is the next-to-last one that is made of silver. It's the coin that is worth 25 cents. The roll for it is colored orange. Having 40 of these in their designated roll adds up to $10. his is considered the most popular coin to have saved up. Even if kids occasionally use it for things like playing pinball or arcade games, it's one of the most common coins ever used for purchasing any specific stuff. Additionally, it is used for things such as parking meters. The quarter is very necessary to have if anyone is going to buy whatever involves a lot of cents in their amounts.

It's the one coin that can ultimately be placed in piggy banks. Having a lot of them saved up will be very useful. The final type of silver coin is the half dollar, which is worth 50 cents but has no paper roll for it. It may be a coin that doesn't appear quite as often as all the other ones. Cash registers in local supermarkets and other primary stores might have them. Even this coin is one worth saving up.

Although it may appear or be given out occasionally, it probably won't be seen all that much. However, keeping this form of coin on hand will be extremely handy for several items that cannot be paid with too small quantities of any or all of the other forms of coins, as well as very little cash alone. At whatever moment, someone who you pay might give you a half dollar when they give you your change if they happen to have any of them stored up.

It's yet another one that is very important to keep with you on hand. Whether it's the copper penny or even the silver nickel, dime, quarter, or half a dollar that will be used for whatever purchases, all forms of coins must be kept safe because even they can get lost or stolen if not secured properly. That's why even rolls for almost every type of coin have been and will continue to be provided by places such as local banks. However, even if anyone wants to cash in their rolls of coins, those will very well need to be handled with extreme care.

Finally, there is the $1 coin, which is made of gold. This form of money may not be available all the time. There is no roll for it either, or it may just appear occasionally. Sometimes, this coin can really come in handy if there are somewhat expensive items that anyone needs to purchase. While they may have their regular groups of cash with them, having it can help pretty much anytime.

Although this is the highest form of coin in U.S. currency, it may not be seen all the time. Some stores may have them in their cash registers, but most of the time, it's just all the other forms of coins that are kept in machines like that. Anyway, now that all the types of these have been discussed, always be sure to have a fair amount in them in your wallet in case banknotes alone can't help you pay for anything specifically that you either want or need.

As mentioned before, storing a lot of them in either piggy banks or rolls can really be of service to everyone, especially if they may want to turn them into cash at places such as any type of financial institution and other locations that can be used for this. Coins have been and will always be very helpful to all people who need to use them for anything minor or even something very important. They are just as valuable as other kinds of American currencies.

Chapter 3
Dollar Bills And Their Details

The next form of American money is the dollar bill. There are a total of 7 types of this form of U.S. currency. The first one is known as the $1 bill, which is also referred to as a single. It has a picture of George Washington on it. This bill is used quite often. Sometimes, more than one of them is spent on items that are not considered too expensive. This amount is equal to the following amounts in coins, which are 100 pennies, 20 nickels, 10 dimes, 4 quarters, and 2 half dollars.

No matter how $1 bills are used or when they are carried in anyone's wallet, it's a form of money that is very common. The next dollar bill is the one that has a value of $2. This is one that has hardly been used or seldom appears anymore. It has the painting of John Trumbull on it. Even if this bill has been produced, most of the time, it has just been kept as a souvenir and doesn't really show up all that much. It may be a bill that is just considered obsolete and is never used to purchase anything.

While it has been given out to some members of the public, perhaps no one may consider spending it at any time. They may just do something such as sticking it to their refrigerator with whatever type of magnet which is used for that appliance.

The next form of a dollar bill is the one that is worth $5 and has a picture of Abraham Lincoln on it. This is one bill that is also used quite often. When $1 bills don't work alone for purchasing slightly higher-priced items, the $5 bill can really come in handy for them. As mentioned before, a full roll of 50 dimes adds up to this amount as well. It's yet another bill that is carried quite often in wallets or even purses.

Even if it has this minor value on it, $5 bills should also be handled very carefully wherever anyone has them stored. Whether they are spent on minor or major things, they are used quite often, just like any form of dollar bills. The fourth type of banknote is the $10 bill. This one has a picture of Alexander Hamilton on it. It is yet another bill that is used quite a lot for whatever items or other things that everyone wants to purchase, or even stuff that is necessary for them to have.

A complete roll of 40 quarters is equal to this amount. It's one value of money that is even used to pay for expensive parking and other things like that. No matter when a dollar bill like this is needed, it must be kept safe in any location where anyone carries it. $10 bills are spent in several places. It's even one that has been used for stuff such as lottery tickets and perhaps scratch-off cards.

The fifth kind of green paper money is the $20 bill. It has the face of Andrew Jackson on the front. $20 bills are a form of money that is used for things that can be a little expensive, such as a lot of groceries.

Even these are ones that must be handled with extreme caution, especially if anyone decides to carry more than one of them. It's one of the forms of payment that has been spent quite a lot. Additionally, they have been used for purchases such as the repairs and cleanings of very important things like cars. A banknote in this amount can be spent at any time, even if it is unexpected.

As previously stated, any type of dollar bill should be set to pay for whatever specific things that anyone needs, and this goes a long way for $20 bills. The next-to-last one is the $50 bill. It has the portrait of President Grant on it. Even if all forms of dollar bills are used, this is one that needs to be handled with a lot of care and safety. Additionally, not too many of these must be carried around in wallets unless absolutely necessary.

This dollar bill can really come in handy for purchases that are very expensive. Moreover, having quite a few of these can even be used for things such as auto and window repairs and replacements. Even if that was mentioned for the $20 bill, a $50 one can be much better. Although every type of dollar bill except the $2 one is used to pay for anything particular or very specific, the $50 one is a bill that can be of a lot of great needs and services, but must be handled with a lot of caution. It does have a high value and is spent quite often on very big purchases and other vital uses.

Perhaps only a quantity of one, two, or three should be kept in wallets. It will be needed at any point in time, but not too many of them must be carried. Even if it is spent just like all the other forms of banknotes, they must be taken care of very carefully. Finally, there is the $100 bill. It is the highest form of cash and has a picture of Benjamin Franklin on it. Out of all the types of paper currency, this one is a bill that must be used with plenty of extreme caution.

Even if it's yet another one that is spent quite often, not too many of those should be carried in wallets or purses unless very necessary. They are ones that are used for the highest type of purchases. Many of these are even kept ready for paying very high bills or other forms of expenses, such as electricity, water, and, above all, rent and mortgages.

Since this is the highest amount in cash and, as mentioned before, it's the one that must be handled with the most extreme care and safety. Now that all the different types of dollar bills have been mentioned along with their many different details, please remember that any or all of them can and will be spent at whatever time they are needed.

Whether they are used for minor purchases or even major and national emergencies, dollar bills are one form of U.S. currency that is very helpful and must always be carried, no matter where anyone goes. Even if no one decides to purchase anything because they may not need it, cash is very crucial to have on hand.

In addition to coins, dollar bills in any amount must be kept ready at even a moment's notice. Each form of it has been and will still be spent on anything that someone primarily wants or very much needs to buy. One extremely important reason to have this is when anyone at all requires any type of specific medicine or pills for whatever kind of sickness or illness they may have. That is something which must be kept in mind.

Money will always be necessary to have for all small and large purchases. No matter which type of dollar bill is used for spending, every form of it must be kept safe and handled with great amount of caution, along with being very careful with them. As mentioned before, both these as well as coins are extremely valuable.

Chapter 4
Methods of Payment In Plastic Form

The ways that anyone chooses to pay for whatever they want and need can be with coins and dollar bills. However, yet another method of purchasing anything at all is with three different types of plastic cards. They are known as debit cards, credit cards, and gift cards. The debit card is used quite often when someone doesn't want to use cash to pay for what they need. At the same time, when any debit card is used to purchase something, the money from that person's bank account is immediately taken out electronically.

No matter how much anyone has in their checking or personal bank account, they must be careful not to use their debit cards too often. Doing something like that can even result in overdrafts on anyone's account when not remembering that they either had a balance in it that was extremely low or nothing at all. While debit cards can be useful for payments of pretty much anything, they must be used and handled very carefully. Those types of cards are one very important key factor associated with anyone's personal or specific bank account.

They can be used occasionally for any minor purchases, but must not be used all the time, even if someone believes that they are perfectly safe for buying anything.

The next form of plastic that is used for spending is the credit card. This one is yet another important one that is related as well as associated with the bank. While anyone can use it for anything they need to have with them, extreme caution must be taken into consideration when any money on it. No matter whether anyone has a credit card for purchasing whatever they want, even if it could be somewhat expensive, they will always have to pay whatever bill arrives for them after using it. Moreover, interest accumulates quite often when this form of payment is used.

While it is very handy to have on hand for any specific purchases that everyone needs, it must not be used too much. The more anyone spends on their credit cards, the higher the bills that they must pay, and getting that done may not be all that easy. Even if everyone carries both debit and credit cards in their wallets and all that, they must be stored as securely as possible. It's very easy to lose them or for someone to steal them and use them for their own purposes.

Along with regular cash and coins, these are utilized for purchasing, but must not be used if anyone either has a very low balance in their account or may not be able to pay whatever high bills they must pay in accordance with whatever amount they used their credit cards for. Finally, there is the ever-popular gift card.

While these can be used to purchase anything that anyone truly wants to have, they must first be purchased at whatever stores feature them anyway. They can have a value anywhere between $20 and $500. Everybody who wants to use gift cards for whatever they want will have to use cash, debit cards, or even credit cards to buy them, along with the amount they want to have them for.

This form of payment can even be presented as a gift for any specific occasion or even if someone wants to just give it to any other person that they love, including a friend or family member. A gift card is a very common method of payment that is used for anything at all, whether it's something expensive or not. As mentioned before, even if anyone chooses to buy something like that, they must be careful in choosing how much they want to pay for it.

Debit cards, credit cards, and gift cards can be used for any specific or minor purchases, but they must be handled very carefully. It can be okay to carry them in wallets and purses, but they can get lost or stolen very easily. Always be sure to keep a close and sharp eye on your many forms of payment, whether they are coins, dollar bills, debit cards, credit cards, or gift cards.

Chapter 5
Checks And Money Orders

Although several types of payment methods have already been discussed, there are a couple of other ones that are associated with American money. One of them is another that relates to the concept and issue of banks and accounts. It is better known as the check. This form of money has quite a bit of information printed on it, such as the following: the home address of the person who has a whole book of checks, the routing and bank account numbers, the number of every check since all of them come in numerical order, and other stuff like that.

As mentioned before, a whole group of checks comes in what is called a checkbook. These are either in one group alone or several groups that are pasted in a folder of the designated bank altogether. The way that someone fills a check out is by writing the date that they will send out the check, the amount for it in a small rectangular box, the name or company that they will be sending it to, the amount of the check-in forms of words, the reason for sending out the check, and of course, their signature.

Each of those has a proper space as well as a line on every check to write with a pen. Pencils must never be used when filling this type of payment out. Additionally, while every check has the extra slip of paper where all the information was first filled out on the original check, a piece of scrap paper or whatever must be placed under it so that no other checks absorb the ink of whatever was written on the first one.

Likewise, when everything is finished, the check must be detached from the book by pulling on it very carefully so that it doesn't rip. Whether these are used for paying any bills or other specific purposes, the amount of them will be withdrawn from the person's bank account in a few days.

The remaining type of money in paper form is called a money order. Those are commonly asked for and given out in post offices or whatever primary stores which have machines that can make them. Although they can be made for any amount that a person wants, a tax amount is included when asking how much he or she wants it for. Money orders, as well as all other methods of payment in the United States, are very common as well as quite popular.

No matter what form of American currency is used for paying anything that is either at low or high prices, each one can and will be used at any specific moment or point in time.

As far as this issue is concerned, all forms of payment that are either in paper, plastic, or metal must be kept ready whenever anyone decides to purchase something minor, specific, or very expensive. They will all come in handy for everything that someone needs to pay, especially if it's a high bill or other expense that has a certain due date and all that.

On the other hand, some small or quite common things that money is used for are food, beverages, household cleaners, any means of oral care, paint for houses, gasoline for vehicles, and anything else that could be considered just minor or for slightly bigger use. Moreover, cash and checks can easily be presented as a gift for any special occasion, such as major holidays like Christmas, as well as birthdays, no matter what types of greeting cards are bought, and someone puts whatever amount of money in them.

Every kind of American currency must be carried in wallets or purses by every man and woman who chooses to go out to any particular or specific place where they plan to purchase whatever they want or need, along with paying important bills. Even when withdrawing any amount of cash from bank accounts, they must be aware of whatever amount they have in those accounts to make sure they don't encounter things like overdrafts or anything else that will result in a negative account balance.

Chapter 6
Important Reasons For Money

Cash, coins, cards, money orders, and checks are used at whatever point in time for any minor purchases or even very required payments. However, now a whole lot of important purposes will be discussed as to why all of these must be kept ready. In addition to paying high bills and other necessary expenses, money must always be on hand for things such as medical emergencies and even when married couples end up with their first child or even more than one child. Even repairs and replacements of windows and doors on cars, houses, and buildings are very costly.

Likewise, the rent and mortgages of homes, as well as apartments, are extremely high and must be paid with anticipation and all that. When anyone wants to buy any specific type of vehicle, whether it is small or big, a lot of payments as well as investments must be made on them. While it will take months or perhaps years to make all of those, plenty of cash, as well as checks, must be saved up to do so. The same goes for any accessories and parts that they need to have installed. There are many expensive things in our country that will require a lot of money to pay for.

This even includes stuff such as furniture and electronics. Additionally, education is something else that money is very necessary for. Things such as school supplies, especially textbooks and notebooks, must be bought right away when classes begin. On the other hand, higher learning institutions such as colleges and universities require large funds to run and operate very efficiently. This even goes for all students who go to places like those.

Every kind of school must have a sufficient budget as well as money provided by many citizens so that every instructor and professor can teach their students all the facts about each specific subject. This is also needed for the printing of things such as the school newspaper and any forms of tests, quizzes, or exams. With more money in cash or even checks supplied to every learning facility, the better they will stay in business. That is truly vital to those who also use computers and other types of electronic equipment.

Even the cleaning of hallways, classrooms, and cafeterias involves American money. Finally, when every semester has concluded, all students who are getting ready to graduate must have the amount they need to order the cap and gown that are required for the actual ceremony. An event like that in school is just as costly as anything else necessary for proper education. On the other hand, money is very much needed for any or all types of charities.

A lot of it must be donated to whichever ones need a big amount of support, and all that. The same is true for auctions featuring whatever specific or minor items that anyone is interested in bidding on or buying right away. Speaking of donations, there are many other nations in the world with poor folks in them, especially children and adults who have no food. This is yet another reason why cash must be kept ready. There are also many people who are homeless and must have someone available who can help them find good and suitable homes.

Moreover, there are even a lot of stray animals and endangered ones around the world, as well as in our own country, that are in critical condition and will need many citizens to provide money for all their special care and protection. No matter what the case may be, every type of American currency not only has primary reasons but very important ones as to why they must be carried on hand as well as always prepared.

Anyway, everyone in the USA will have small or big things that they want to purchase or are required to have, along with all types of expenses and bills that they need to pay by a certain due date that are on them. Each payment method must be set up right away.

Chapter 7
Conclusion

Although many concepts and issues on the theme and topic of American money have been discussed, mentioned, and described in a lot of different details, there are still some tips and pointers that must be kept in mind when dealing with it and spending it. For example, no matter how many personal, important, and online transactions that everyone decides to do, very big amounts of money must never be spent on any of them unless it's absolutely necessary.

However, while cash and checks are the most common ways of paying things like bills and other debts, all forms of payment are also used for traveling purposes, including field trips from school, business trips, and vacations that can be extremely expensive. Speaking of which, anyone who must get to a certain, specific, or much-needed place or destination that is somewhat or very far away from where they currently are but cannot use their own car to do so needs to carry a good amount of cash with them for going on long trips either in or on public modes of transportation such as taxis, buses, or trains.

Two other matters to take into consideration when handling or spending money are gambling and betting. The first action is done a lot in casinos that have slot machines, tables with a roulette wheel, and tables that use dice, poker chips, and, of course, playing cards. The other one is done most frequently at racetracks when anyone makes bets on a racehorse, that they truly believe is the fastest one and can win very easily. Nobody should ever gamble using all the money that they carry with them or even with any of their other valuables, like jewelry.

No one at all must ever make bets or wagers with all the cash they have on hand, and not even with any of their property of great importance, including cars and entire houses. Doing so will result in and spell out a huge and painful disaster for them if everything ends up lost. Anyone can do these occasionally if they believe they are capable of handling it. The same goes for the lottery.

Even if somebody must be the proper age to play it, they must do so very responsibly. However, after whatever tickets are bought and before the results are officially announced, whoever does play the lottery may soon realize that they are not as lucky or even close to winning it as they think. Other than that, a very terrifying thing that money has been and is still used for is all types of real weapons. No normal person must ever buy any because each one of them has been classified and categorized as lethal, deadly, and extremely dangerous.

If anyone decides to purchase a primary one, such as a handgun or revolver, it must only be used for complete and total protection. Although bulletproof vests can also be bought for more shielding against firearms, those might not work all the time. Additionally, hunters who spend cash on weapons, including shotguns, rifles, and knives, for their hunting trips involving things such as duck season and deer season, must be very careful with handling them.

Even while waiting to fire at wild animals like grizzly bears, there are some hunters who have been accidentally killed by other hunters who carelessly shoot at anything that moves. Moreover, very important people, including the police, have used their money to keep themselves equipped with not only their firearms but also handcuffs, clubs, and patrol cars that they need for capturing, apprehending, and arresting all notorious criminals.

Another crimefighting facility with weapons is the FBI, which has utilized its money on those. Likewise, much bigger and more important groups of people, such as the army, navy, or air force, have invested cash in not just surplus and weaponry but also their many types of combat vehicles, which are mostly tanks, battleships, and fighter jets. Regarding the various minor, important, special, and dangerous reasons in this book as to why money needs to be spent, every citizen must be aware of them.

Each person must also keep a very close watch on all the forms and methods of payment they use while keeping them as secure and safe as possible. In addition to that, before going out, they must also be extremely careful in deciding what amount in cash and coins, as well as the number of plastic cards and checks that they want to carry. Any of these can get lost or stolen if they are not handled properly.

All United States banks need to keep track of both their own money that they keep in vaults as well as the cash and cents that are in all their customers' accounts. For a lot more protection, plenty of security guards must always be present or available in banks because even robberies can occur at any time. As far as the central theme of this story, which is American money, goes, all bits of information that say how and why it is spent and must also be kept not only very secure but also prepared all the time have been discussed.

To finish it up in a more pleasant way, I have chosen to add a very special bonus feature. It is a set of two poems from my first book that elaborate a little bit on the main idea of the second one that I have just written. Please read them very carefully, and all of you will completely understand why each form and method of payment has been and still is considered as truly important as ever. Everyone can and will always realize that. Here they are for your entire viewing pleasure.

Bonus Feature

Great Poem About Money

Money, money, don't go away
When vanishing, you make us blue
Your green has always made our day
And so have you

You come in coins and bills
Our destiny comes upon your sight
With you gone, it's like us taking sleeping pills
It becomes your duty to make things right

Dollar, quarter, nickel, penny, or dime
You make us smile
Always having you handy, it's our great old time
We love stacking you pile after pile

Your value has always been a treasure
We adore you for what you are
It has always been our pleasure
Whether you come from near or far

Money, money, you're ours to keep
Our lives have depended on you
Please don't go or we'll weep
That I say is definitely true

You will always be for who is needy
Poor ones will rely on you
Never be with those who are greedy
Common people speak all this, too

Amazing Poem About The Lottery

The lottery from every state is our biggest prize
There are many different amounts to win
Money won from here is in any size
Hitting the jackpot can indicate a huge grin

Odds for this are millions to one
Various tickets are played each day
Every variety can trigger much fun
Those who win big can yell hooray

All moments with these releases a load of cash
People celebrate with victory and cheer
Along with running out in a quick flash
Whether they come from far or near

Winning the lottery is meant for many joys
It will be spread out day and night
For all men, ladies, girls, and boys
And is considered a very happy sight